Measure It with Math!

MEASURING TIME

Anne O'Daly

PowerKiDS press

Published in 2024 by The Rosen Publishing Group, Inc.
2544 Clinton Street, Buffalo, NY 14224

Portions of this work were originally authored by Chris Woodford and published as *Time*.
All new material this edition authored by Anne O'Daly.

Children's Publisher: Anne O'Daly

Design Manager: Keith Davis

Picture Manager: Sophie Mortimer

Picture credits:

Key: t = top, tr = top right, b = bottom

Front Cover: Shutterstock: Kaspars Grinvalds tl, Marques l, Tito Onz r, pukach tr.

Interior: iStock: 3DSculptor 21, aislan13 27t, Bet Noire 26, danaibe12 8, frentusha 10, Maria Ponomariova 7, redhumv 27b; Library of Congress: 20; Public Domain: Racklever 17; Shutterstock: Elena11 4, Robin Gentry 13, Gitanna 16, lucadp 24, Jacob Lund 25, Andrii Rudyk 14, Pixel-Shot 11, Sangaron 6, Janez Volmajer 1, 18.

Cataloging-in-Publication Data

Names: O'Daly, Anne.
Title: Measuring time / Anne O'Daly.
Description: New York : Powerkids Press, 2024. | Series: Measure it with math! | Includes glossary and index.
Identifiers: ISBN 9781642827880 (pbk.) | ISBN 9781642827897 (library bound) | ISBN 9781642827903 (ebook)
Subjects: LCSH: Time--Juvenile literature. | Time measurements--Juvenile literature.
Classification: LCC QB209.5 O34 2024 | DDC 529--dc23

Manufactured in the United States of America

CPSIA Compliance Information: Batch #CSPK24. For further information contact Rosen Publishing at 1-800-237-9932.

Contents

What Is Time?

Time is how we measure the speed at which everything ages. We can't see time, but it is always there. We use watches, clocks, and calendars to mark the passing of time.

Earth, Moon, and Sun

How we measure time comes from the way Earth, the moon, and the sun move in the sky. It takes a year for Earth to circle the sun. It takes a month for the moon to move around Earth. Earth is also spinning slowly. It takes 24 hours for Earth to spin once. When the place on Earth where we are living faces the sun, we say it is daytime. When our part of Earth faces away from the sun, we say it is nighttime.

It takes about a month for the moon to move around Earth. The moon's shape appears to change during this time. A thin slice is called a crescent moon. A full circle is called a full moon.

WINTER AND SUMMER

Earth turns around an imaginary line called an axis. As Earth moves around the sun, the Northern Hemisphere, or northern half of Earth, tilts toward the sun at certain times of the year. It tilts away from the sun at other times of the year. In summer, the Northern Hemisphere faces toward the sun. There are more hours of daylight, and the sunlight is stronger and warmer.

FACT

One year is usually 365 days. But every fourth year has 366 days. When this happens, the year is called a leap year.

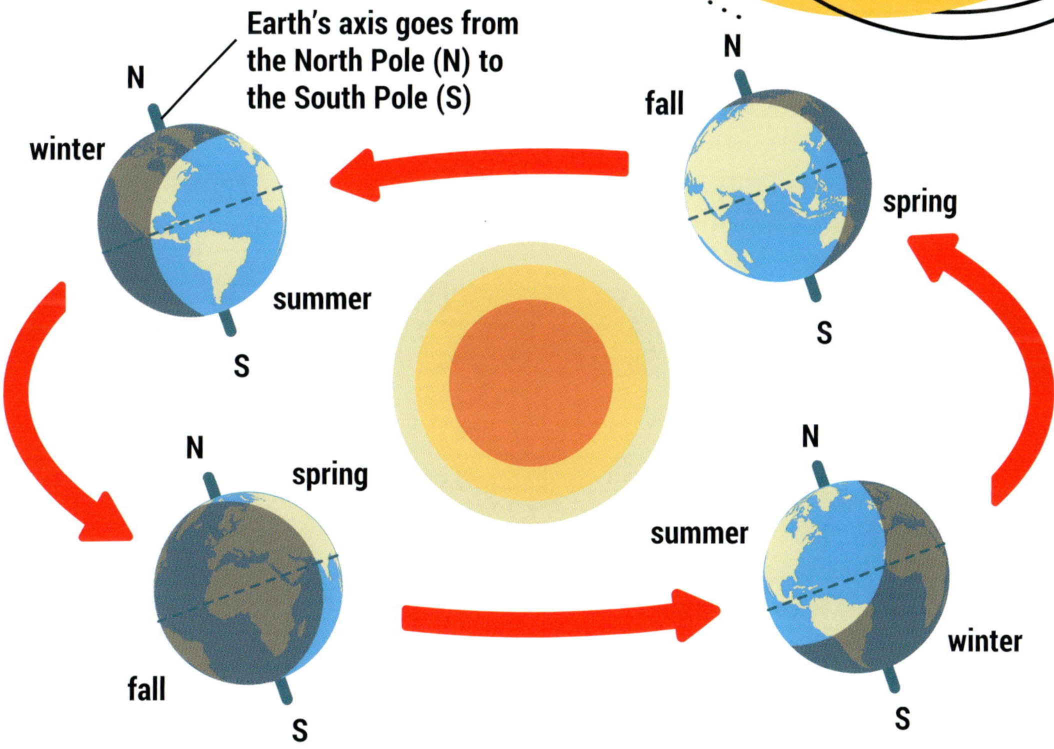

Units of Time

Time never stops. So that we can measure it, we divide time into units, or pieces. A millennium is the name we give to 1,000 years. As well as years, we divide time into smaller units such as months, weeks, days, hours, minutes, and seconds.

Smaller Units

We can divide each of the units of time into even smaller units. There are 12 months in a year, just over four weeks in a month, and seven days in a week. A day can be divided into 24 hours. An hour has 60 minutes. One minute has 60 seconds. A second has 1,000 milliseconds.

Most clocks measure hours, minutes, and seconds. The short hand moves slowly to mark the hours. The longer hand moves faster to mark off the minutes. The long, thin second hand moves around to mark every second.

TRY THIS

PASSING TIME

Enter the missing periods of time (**?**) in this list:

15 billion years = the age of the universe

4.5 billion years = the age of Earth

80 years = average lifetime of a person

22 months = time it takes for a baby elephant to grow inside its mother

? months = the number of months in a year

? days = time it takes for Earth to circle the sun

8 hours = the amount of sleep most adults need

? seconds = the number of seconds in an hour

8 minutes = the time it takes for light to travel from the sun to Earth

1 second = beat of a human heart

Answers on page 32.

Many people live for almost 80 years. A person passes through babyhood, childhood, and adulthood in that time.

Ancient Time

The ancient Egyptians used the position of the sun to tell them the time. They invented a clock called a sundial. The round dial was divided into 12 units, the hours. When the sun shone on the face of the sundial, a pointer cast a shadow across it. As the sun moved, the shadow moved around the dial, like the hour hand on a clock. Sundials still exist today.

STONEHENGE

Stonehenge is a circle of huge stones in England. It is about 4,000 years old. On the morning of the longest day of the year, June 21, the sun rises in line with some of the stones. Scientists think that ancient people used Stonehenge as a clock or calendar.

HOURGLASS
It takes exactly one hour for the sand to trickle from the top to the bottom of this hourglass.

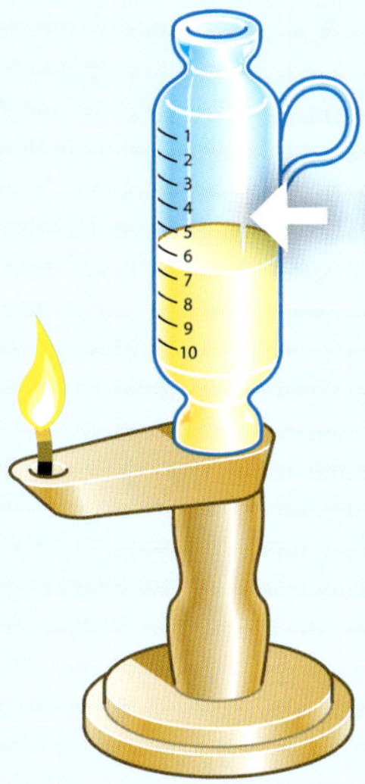

OIL CLOCK
People could tell the time using an oil clock by the amount of oil that burned away in the lamp.

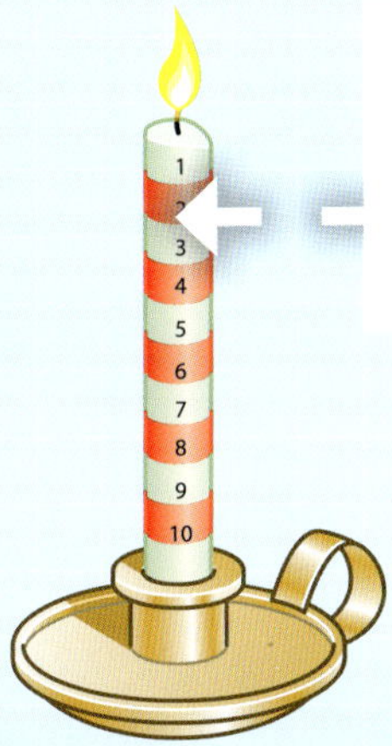

CANDLE CLOCK
As a candle clock burned down, people could count the number of hours that had passed.

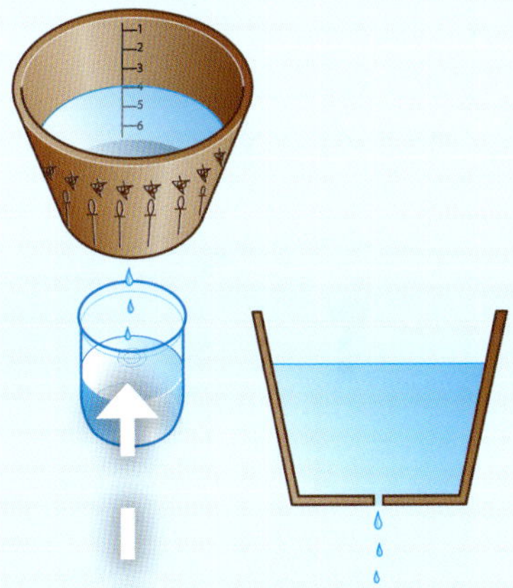

Other Ancient Clocks

Sundials only work if the sun is shining. Ancient people used other ways to tell time. In an hourglass, a fixed amount of sand takes exactly one hour to trickle from the top half into the bottom half. People measured the passing of time by turning the hourglass over every hour.

EGYPTIAN WATER CLOCK
Water drips slowly from a hole in a pot and shows how many hours have passed.

Keeping Track of Time

Calendars count the days passing through a year. The first calendars were created nearly 2,500 years ago in Babylon (now part of Iraq). People saw there were about 29.5 days between one full moon and the next full moon. They called this time period a month.

The Aztecs lived in Mexico many hundreds of years ago. They kept track of important dates using the Aztec Calendar Stone. This stone measures about 13 feet (4 meters) across.

TRY THIS

READ A CALENDAR

This calendar page shows the days of the week. They are arranged in columns. It shows that the third Monday in the month is January 16.

What is the date of the second Tuesday in the month?

What is the date of the third Friday in the month?

Answers on page 32.

JANUARY 2023

SU	MO	TU	WE	TH	FR	SA
1	2	3	4	5	6	7
8	9	10	11	12	13	14
15	16	17	18	19	20	21
22	23	24	25	26	27	28
29	30	31				

Egyptian Calendar

The Babylonian year had 12 months, or 354 days. But a year really has 365 days. The ancient Egyptians came up with a more accurate calendar. They used the sun. They figured out the time it took Earth to move around the sun. They called that time a year. The year was divided into 12 months. A month had 30 days. The ancient Egyptians added five extra days to the end of the year to make 365 days.

FACT

The earliest record of a seven-day week was in Babylon in 600 B.C.E. A holy day was celebrated every seven days.

Galileo's Pendulum

Early clocks such as sundials were not very practical to use. The brilliant Italian scientist Galileo Galilei discovered pendulums in 1583. A pendulum is a long bar with a heavy weight at one end. Galileo thought the movement of a pendulum could be used in clocks.

SWINGING PENDULUMS

A swinging pendulum always takes the same amount of time to swing backward and forward. That makes it a useful way to tell time.

Each time a pendulum swings, it travels the same distance to either side (**2** and **3**) of its starting point (**1**). As it slows, the pendulum swings less far, but the distance between **1** and **2** is always the same as the distance between **1** and **3**.

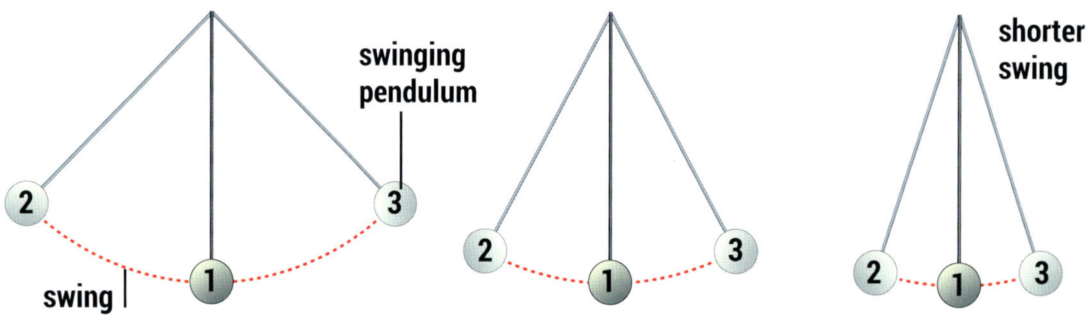

TRY THIS

TIMING THE SWINGS

A complete swing of a pendulum is the time it takes to get back to its starting position (from **2** to **3** and back to **2** again in the diagram on page 12).

* If a pendulum makes one full swing every 2 seconds, how many will it make in 1 minute?
* If it takes 3 seconds to make a full swing, how many swings will it make in 1 minute?

Answers on page 32.

A swing works in the same way as a pendulum. A person on a swing will move backward and forward in a regular pattern.

FACT

The world's biggest pendulum clock is in Japan. It is nearly 42 feet (12.8 m) across.

Time and Motion

Gravity is the force that makes things fall toward Earth. It keeps Earth and other planets moving around the sun. Gravity also makes a pendulum swing. Galileo suggested using a swinging pendulum to control how a clock works. He got the idea while he watched a lamp swinging from the roof of a cathedral. He timed the swings using the pulse in his wrist. He found the lamp always took exactly the same time to move backward and forward.

Pendulum Clocks

Pendulum clocks have lots of moving parts. Gears are wheels with teeth cut into their edges. They make the hands of a clock turn. The swinging pendulum controls how fast the gears move. Power comes from a slowly falling weight, but the pendulum may change length slightly if the weather is hot or cold. Then the clock will run too fast or too slow.

Clockmakers found another way to power clocks. They used springs instead of a falling weight. Springs are small coils of wire. They keep a clock ticking at the same rate as they unwind.

An old pendulum clock

MECHANICAL PARTS

When a pendulum swings, it rocks a lever called a pallet. This lifts up and down once every second. It makes a "tick-tock" noise. As the pallet moves, it turns the escape wheel. This is connected by gears to other wheels, including the main wheel.

FALLING WEIGHT

The main wheel has a heavy weight fixed to it that slowly moves down. The falling weight powers the clock by turning the main wheel. The main wheel then turns the other gears. The swinging pendulum controls the movement of the gears, which turn the hands around the dial. The clock has to be wound regularly to raise the weight back up toward the barrel.

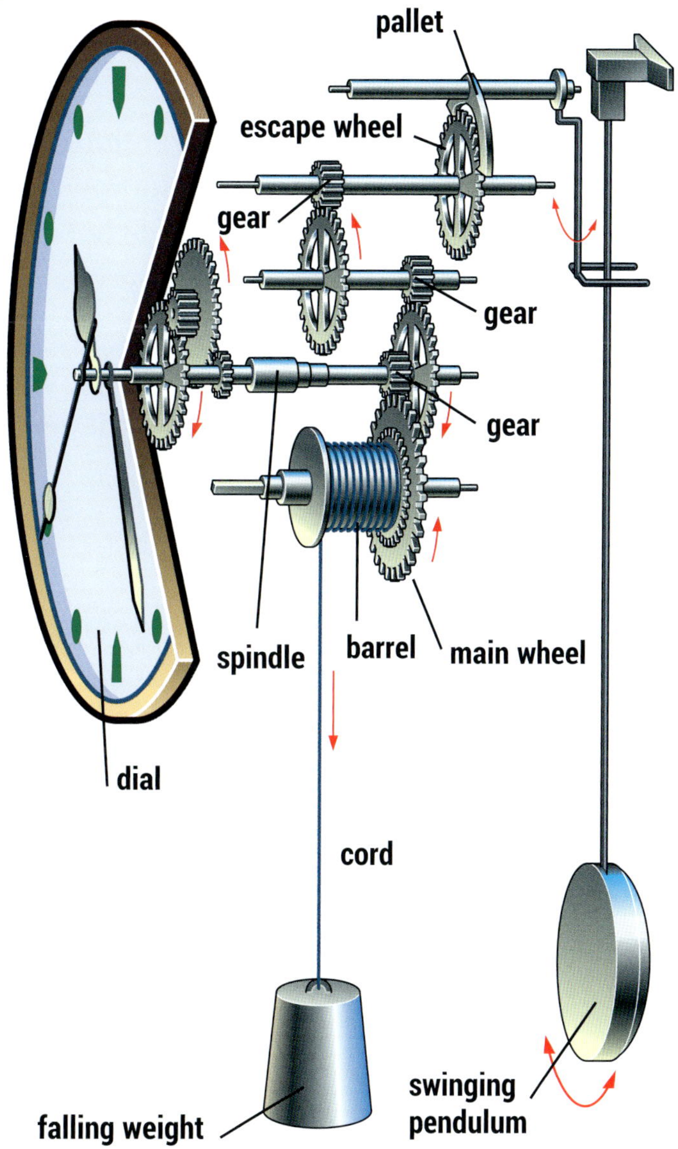

Small Clocks and Watches

For a long time after their invention, clocks were large. They were also expensive. Not many people could afford to buy them. They were expensive because clockmakers cut each gear wheel by hand. They were large because of the space needed for the pendulum.

This clockmaker is using tweezers to adjust the tiny moving parts in a watch.

FACT

Some expensive modern watches have more than 200 small parts inside them.

The invention of springs allowed clocks to be made without pendulums and falling weights. This meant smaller clocks and pocket watches could be made. In 1841, a British engineer named Joseph Whitworth invented a machine that could cut gears. Small clocks and watches could be made more quickly. Soon they were made in factories. These clocks and watches were cheaper, so more people could buy them.

SEA CLOCKS

Early mechanical clocks worked well on land. But they could not be used on ships. At sea, the movement of the waves made it impossible for a pendulum to swing properly. In the 1730s, British clockmaker John Harrison solved the problem. He designed accurate sea watches that were driven by special springs. One was a large pocket watch. It lost only five seconds during a sea voyage from England to Jamaica in 1762.

This is one of the sea watches designed by John Harrison.

Time Zones

Only one side of Earth faces the sun at any one time. This means it is daytime on one side of the world while it is nighttime on the other side. People all over the world agree on the time using time zones. The world is divided into 24 time zones. People living in each zone have their own time.

Greenwich Mean Time

International time is set by the standard time at Greenwich in England. The time there is called Greenwich Mean Time (GMT). People living in zones east of Greenwich have later times than GMT. People living in time zones west of Greenwich have earlier times.

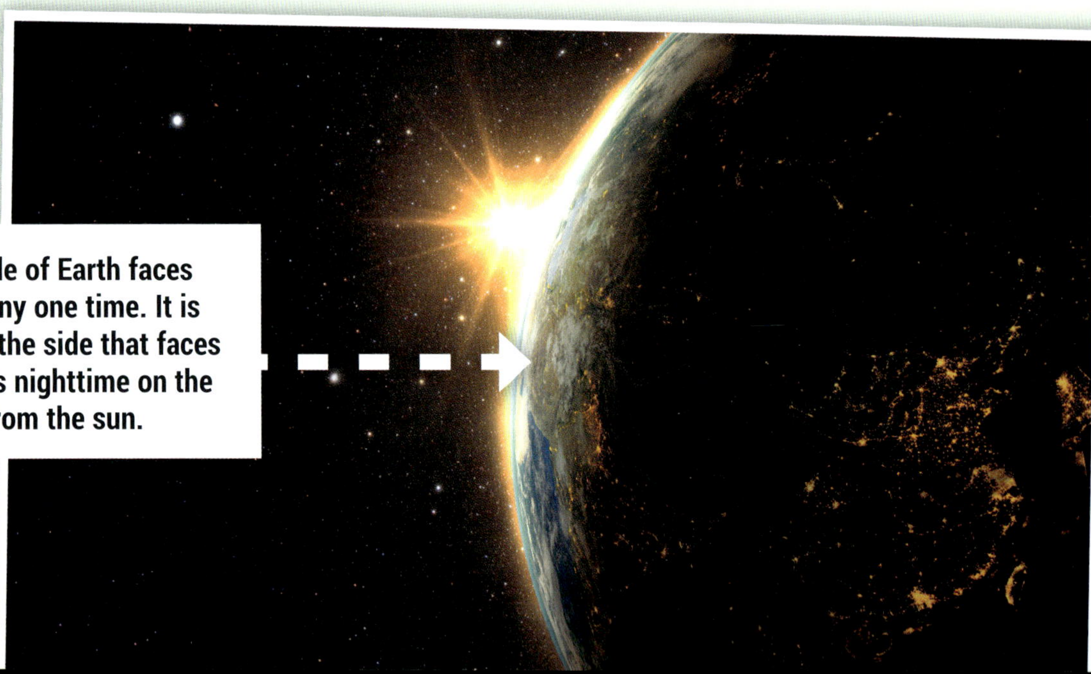

Only one side of Earth faces the sun at any one time. It is daytime on the side that faces the sun. It is nighttime on the side away from the sun.

Ocean to Ocean

North America is a big continent. It has five different time zones. The time is always three hours later in the day for New Yorkers than it is for Californians. That is because the sun always rises earlier over New York than over California.

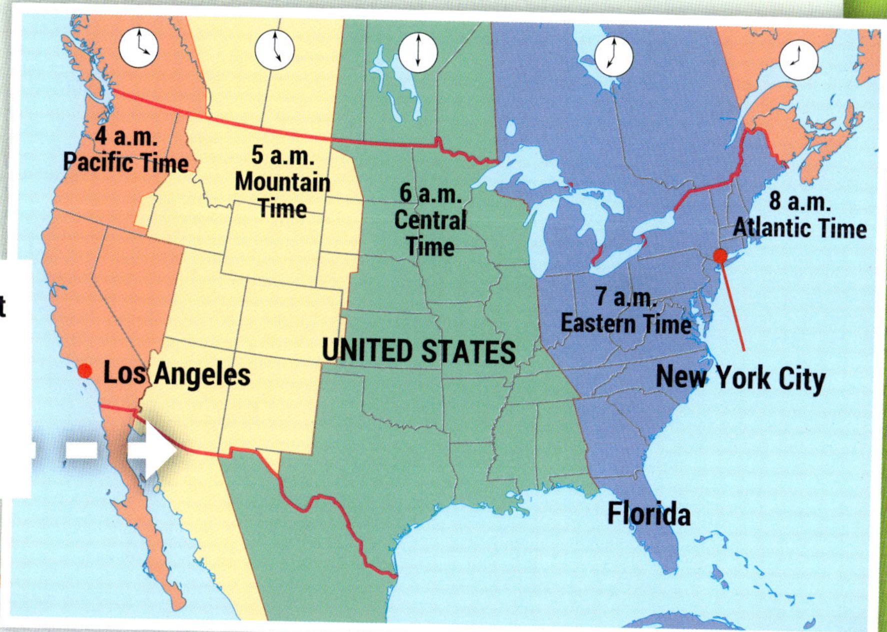

North America has five different time zones. When it is 7 a.m. in New York City, it is 4 a.m. in Los Angeles, California.

TRY THIS

TIME IN NORTH AMERICA

Look at the map above and work out the time in different places.

* When it is 12:00 noon in New York City, what time is it in Los Angeles?
* When it is 4 p.m. in Los Angeles, what time is it in New York City?
* When it is 8 a.m. in New York City, what time is it in Florida?

Answers on page 32.

How Fast Is Time?

Time almost always passes at the same speed. But the brilliant scientist Albert Einstein showed that sometimes time speeds up or slows down. The faster an object travels through space, the slower it travels through time.

The Speed of Light

Light travels at the speed of 186,000 miles (298,000 km) each second. What would happen if we could sit on a beam of light and zoom along with it? Einstein said time would pass more slowly for us than it would for people not moving so fast.

The scientist Albert Einstein. He showed that time does not always pass at the same speed.

FACT

In water, the speed of time is slower. Water has more mass than air. This means time passes a little slower underwater.

He also said that as the pull of gravity gets stronger, time passes more slowly.

The Theory of Relativity

These ideas of Einstein are called the theory of relativity. They made people think about time and space in new ways.

Time passes slightly faster on a rocket when it orbits Earth than it does on the ground.

TRY THIS

SPEED AND TIME

Light travels 186,000 miles (298,000 km) in 1 second.

* How far will light travel in 10 seconds?
* How far will light travel in 1 minute?
* How long will it take a beam of light to travel from a star 3,720,000 miles (5,960,000 km) away?

Answers on page 32.

The Ages of Time

Clocks tell us what time it is. Calendars track days, months, and years. But longer periods of time are harder to count. Fossils are the remains of long-dead creatures that have turned to stone. How do we know how old they are?

Carbon Dating

In 1947, American scientist Willard Frank Libby figured out how old something was by measuring how much carbon it contained. He called his method carbon dating. It works for things that are up to 60,000 years old. It does not work for fossils that are millions of years old. Radioactive elements are used to find out their ages.

CARBON CLOCK

Everything that has ever lived contains some carbon. It is the black material in coal and in pencil "lead." Over thousands of years, one kind of carbon changes into another kind of carbon. This happens very slowly but at a steady rate. By measuring the different amounts of carbon present in living or dead things, scientists can figure out how old something is.

FACT

The oldest fossils found so far are 3.5 billion years old. They were found in western Australia.

HOW A FOSSIL FORMS

1. Millions of years ago, a dinosaur dies next to a river.

2. The flesh of the dinosaur rots away until only the bones are left. The river covers the bones in mud.

3. The bones are gradually covered by layers of rocks over millions of years. The bones turn to stone.

4. The fossil is found when the rocks wear away. Scientists use a process called radiometric dating to work out how old the fossil is.

Modern Time

Modern clocks and watches run on batteries, or electric power. A tiny battery makes the electricity that keeps the watch going. Tiny pieces of quartz are used in some clocks and watches. Quartz is a type of crystal. When electricity flows into it, the pieces of quartz shake backward and forward at a steady speed. This shaking action is used to keep track of time.

This modern smartwatch has a digital display showing the time at 10:12, along with the day of the week, the month, and the date.

FACT

Pure quartz is also called silicon dioxide. It is made of atoms of silicon and oxygen.

DIGITAL DISPLAYS

Some watches and clocks have moving hands. Others are digital. Digital clocks and watches show the time with numbers, or digits. They often have a built-in stopwatch and alarm clock. Some digital watches also show the time in different countries. There is usually a piece of quartz crystal in a digital watch to keep time.

Athletes are timed by a trainer using a digital stopwatch.

Quartz Clocks and Watches

It takes very little energy to make quartz move. The battery in a quartz watch lasts for many years. The first quartz clock was made in 1928 by engineers Warren Marrison and Joseph Horton at the Bell Laboratories in New York. The first quartz wristwatch was launched in Japan in 1969. Three years later the first watch with a digital display was produced by the Hamilton Watch Company of Pennsylvania. The first watches that could download information from computers went on sale in the 1990s.

Other Clocks

Ancient peoples kept track of time by looking at the skies. In the last few hundred years clockmakers have invented other ways of measuring time. But how will people measure time in the future?

A car's navigation unit tracks distance and time. The display shows how far the car is from its destination, and how long it will take to get there.

FACT

The kurinji plant has a slow-running biological clock. The plant flowers only once every 12 years!

TIME IN NATURE

People have a built-in sense of time. We get hungry or sleepy at certain times without looking at clocks. This is called our biological clock. Scientists think our biological clocks are driven by proteins. Proteins are the chemicals from which our bodies are made. In the future, scientists are sure to find out more about biological clocks and their importance.

Flowers only bloom at certain times of the year. This is a kind of biological clock.

Atomic Clocks

The most accurate way of telling the time is with an atomic clock. It works like a quartz clock, but instead of quartz it uses atoms. Atoms are so small we cannot see them. They give off pulses of energy 10 billion times every second. The atomic clock counts these pulses to work out and show the time. This type of clock is very accurate. Scientists say that an atomic clock built in 2022 will lose just one second every 300 billion years!

HANDS ON

Make a Sundial

WHAT YOU NEED

* A dinner plate about 10 inches (25 cm) across
* A sharp pencil
* A piece of thin cardboard about 12 inches (30 cm) by 12 inches (30 cm)
* Modeling clay
* Scissors

WHAT YOU DO

1. Put the plate on top of the cardboard. Draw around the edge of the plate to make a circle on the cardboard.

2. Cut out the circle using the scissors. Ask an adult to help.

Your Finished Sundial

Once you have drawn the hour lines for noon, 3 p.m., 6 p.m. and 9 a.m., you can figure out where the other hour lines go by dividing each quarter of the circle into equal thirds.

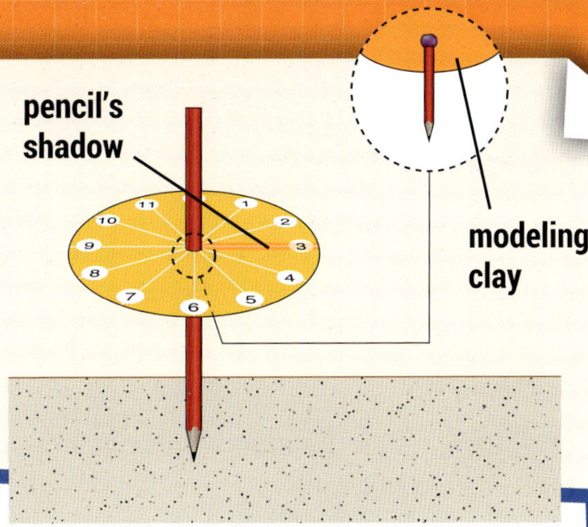

3. Figure out roughly where the center of the circle is. Make a small pencil mark at that point.

4. Put a small ball of modeling clay on the underside of the cardboard circle, beneath the pencil mark.

5. Carefully push the pencil through the center of the cardboard so it goes through into the modeling clay. Ask an adult to help you. Try not to bend the cardboard.

6. Place your sundial on the ground outside. Choose somewhere that is sunny all day.

7. At noon, draw a straight line where the shadow of the pencil falls. Do the same at 3 p.m. and 6 p.m. Draw another line at 9 a.m.

Glossary

atom A tiny particle of a substance.

atomic clock A very accurate clock that tells time using the tiny movements of atoms.

biological clock An animal's or plant's built-in sense of time.

calendar A way of keeping track of the days, weeks, and months in a year.

carbon dating A way of finding out the age of very old things.

digital watch A watch that shows the time with numbers, not hands.

escape wheel The main driving wheel in a pendulum clock.

gear A pair of interlocking wheels with teeth around their edges. The wheels turn at different speeds depending on how many teeth each has.

gravity A force that pulls things toward Earth.

mechanical clock A clock that is made of moving parts, such as gears, pendulums, and springs.

millennium A period of time that lasts for 1,000 years.

month The approximate time it takes for the moon to go once around Earth.

pendulum A swinging bar that helps keep time in a mechanical clock.

quartz clock A modern clock that uses the tiny vibrations of the mineral quartz (silicon dioxide) to keep time.

relativity A theory of the scientist Albert Einstein; in relativity, time slows down when people travel at very high speeds.

spring A spiral of wire that powers a mechanical clock.

sundial A device that measures time using changing shadows.

time zone A region of the world that has the same time.

year The time it takes for Earth to move once around the sun (365 days).

Find Out More

BOOKS

Askew, Mike
Let's Measure It. You Can Master Math.
Rosen Publishing, 2022.

Dorling Kindersley.
How to Measure Everything.
Dorling Kindersley, 2018.

Monster Math
(Four Volumes)
Lerner Publishing, 2020.

Rustad, Martha E. H.
Measuring Time.
Capstone Publishing, 2019.

WEBSITES

www.mathsisfun.com/time-zones-world.html
Information and graphics on world time zones. Includes links to other pages on clocks and Earth's orbit.

www.ducksters.com/science/physics/theory_of_relativity.php
Basic introduction to Einstein's Theory of Relativity from Ducksters.

www.thoughtco.com/what-is-time-4156799
Simple definition and explanation of time from Thoughtco.com.

www.mathsisfun.com/leap-years.html
An explanation of leap years from Math Is Fun.

Index

ANSWERS

Page 7: 12; 365 (366 in a leap year); 3,600. **Page 11:** January 10; January 20. **Page 13:** 30; 20. **Page 19:** 9 a.m.; 7 p.m.; 8 a.m. **Page 21:** 1,860,000 miles (2,980,000 km); 11,160,000 miles (17,880,000 km); 20 seconds.